Ode to Not Knowing

poems by

Maria Tori

Finishing Line Press
Georgetown, Kentucky

Ode to Not Knowing

For Hanah and Georgia

Copyright © 2023 by Maria Tori
ISBN 979-8-88838-172-4 First Edition
All rights reserved under International and Pan-American Copyright Conventions. No part of this book may be reproduced in any manner whatsoever without written permission from the publisher, except in the case of brief quotations embodied in critical articles and reviews.

ACKNOWLEDGMENTS

"Clawfoot Tub" first appeared in *Poetry East*
"Your House, A Room" first appeared in *The Louisville Review*

Publisher: Leah Huete de Maines
Editor: Christen Kincaid
Cover Art: Maria Tori
Author Photo: Tom Downs
Cover Design: Elizabeth Maines McCleavy

Order online: www.finishinglinepress.com
　　　　　also available on amazon.com

　　　　　　　Author inquiries and mail orders:
　　　　　　　　　Finishing Line Press
　　　　　　　　　　PO Box 1626
　　　　　　　　Georgetown, Kentucky 40324
　　　　　　　　　　　　USA

Table of Contents

Tea From Leonardtown 1

The Truth About God 2

Ode to Not Knowing 3

Nuthatch, White-Breasted 4

Gutter Water 5

Dear Apis 7

The Suddenness 11

The Last Month 12

Cockroach 13

A State of Being Near Nightfall 14

Twilight: Civil, Nautical, Astronomical 15

Your House, A Room 16

Portrait of a Life, Yesterday 17

I Must Lay Back Into This World 18

It is so beautiful here 19

Clawfoot Tub 20

Untitled 22

*"My barn having burned to the ground,
I can now see the moon."*
—Mizuta Masahide

Tea From Leonardtown

Today, I drink the tea I stole from the woman's house in Maryland.

I saved it to heal me like those hills and birds and so much distance
between me and my real life ought to.
To remind me of that room I'd rented and the hope
of peace and loveliness that came to me in the mix of eccentric
books and so many posters of Monet, and people like him.
Every pattern of blanket laying against
the other and telling me the truth.

Today, I drink the tea.

I am lost. I am trapped amongst the boxwood hedge overgrown
in my body and mind. Like walls—effortless walls you can *just* see
   through.
Shoving your face in is hard enough.

The tea is good. There is a bug in it. Instead of fishing him out of the
cup, I swallow him whole like medicine.
What answers will he give me?
I'm out here with my maps looking for places to go. Avenues to turn
   down—
ordering atlases to other places, Portuguese dictionaries from the
   bookstore—
things I cannot afford.

Making up time (and reasons), time until my birthday.
Time until I have to make decisions
I don't want to have to make or unmake. How many miles until
Leonardtown? How long can I make a cup of tea last?
What happens if I waste it?

Like I often do. On the windowsill, on the table,
the kitchen counter. Sitting on the edge of the porch,
for the birds, maybe.

The Truth About God

Birds everywhere are icing over.

Tails freezing
bodies freezing
and death.

Somewhere it's warm,
but not here.

I watched geese honking
and playing in the pond—

Don't they know it's so cold out here?

Would the time they had
on the pond be worth it
if they couldn't wake up in morning,

Their wings plastered to their breasts and
nothing in between?

The dancing in the water,
the singing and intensity of being so awake—

Feathery bodies spinning
like dancers in a music box.

The birds and death play back
and forth—

God must have been a bird,
Cold and Dancing.

Ode To Not Knowing

*I can hear the loons crying out across the lake.
It is night, and there is a full moon. I crouch at
the tree line listening. Aching toward their calls.
I know them.*

I must hear a loon cry,
like so many before me have,
and like so many others have not.

Somewhere, there is a child,
or one buried inside an adult,
who has never known such a thing as a loon.
Who does not know that they cry.

To not know that they dive into the water
carving stark, rolling lines with their bodies
to catch fish and play.

To not know the beauty of so much black
and white—those red-eyes.

To not know that somewhere in that loon,
in that fish, in that water, is my body,
un-tempted and not lost. I am with them.

To not know one's own being.
Until pushed,
       I must be at the shores.

Suddenly, like the leap of a whale—
the loon cries.

Nuthatch, White-Breasted

There is a knot in the tree where once it had been injured.
Or maybe just born that way.
There are two holes in that knot just smaller than my fist.
There is a bird, a nuthatch, white-breasted.

He comes
folding around the bark, rotating
his little body like a whirly-gig beetle in the water.
He's slower, with direction and purpose.

He stops himself at the knot, looking inside one of the holes.
His whole body fits inside. He makes use of this.
He does not hesitate, like I would. To be headfirst into the dark.
I wonder, just for his sake alone, what would lie beyond
to injure him?

A curiosity must confound him—
so drives his little body inside the opening,
so drives mine. He tosses bits of stick out of the hole,
looking after them as they fall. Did he drop one by accident?

He doesn't think about it long. Just long enough to know it's gone.
When he moves, he offers bleated chirps of effort, they are soft.
You must lean in to notice. You wonder, *is it him?*
And then, you know that it is.

The day goes along after this. I do not see him,
though I look. Just long enough to know he is gone.

I wonder,
does he think of making a home here?

I wonder,
why am I afraid to wander into the dark?

Gutter Water

I am a great lover of all things.

I love fully, openly, and wisely.
Without time and without hope.

I am so full, I could
easily be twisted.

Surely, just like you, I have thought
about the excitement that comes
right before, and after, death.

Choices away from being either one:
lover grounded/lover descended.

Surely I am not the only one
who thinks of playing God.

I thought of it today, walking home
after work. Drinking a warm coffee,
letting the rain fall without despair
onto my head.

My dog ate up a cicada and I heard it
scream all the way down her throat until
it didn't anymore.

I scolded her, how dare she take a life
that wasn't hers to take—especially with so
many already dead on the ground. Couldn't
she just be satisfied by one of those?

But how could I blame her?
Thinking after all, about that
pound of energy, buzzing, breathing,
living—
until it's not anymore.

In the silence, as we mourn, the sound
of gutter water tapping into a storm drain.

Dear Apis

I picked up a honeybee off my kitchen floor,
sure that she was dying.

Mostly, she slept. Her left foot twitched.
Occasionally, she would get a fever to clean herself
and so she would, frantically.

At one moment,
she tried to fly.

Her body—fatigue.
It was hard to lift herself up.
I felt her vibrating off my skin,
into the air.

She tumbled short distances,
and, in courage, took off again.
She landed in some water
at the base of an empty pot.
I rescued her.

I watched her body move
with her breath, her heartbeat.
I was sure she would die in my hand.

I agreed to hold her as long as that would take.

Though I got impatient.
Thinking of writing about her death
before it had happened. Thinking of
taking a walk later.

In my thoughts,
she must have felt my distance,
suddenly she didn't want me anymore.

Before, when I had tried to give her refuge
on a flower, then a leaf,
She refused.
Seeking comfort, seeking hive-mind.

Seeking hand.

Now, she stumbled off idle and
sour onto some red leaf lettuce.

For a while, she fumbled
along the edges.

Eventually, she fell to the bottom
of the planter.

        Is it my fault I walked away?

Too dampened by the reasons for living to
stop for death…
or perhaps to weary to wait for it?

Maybe it was the not knowing.
Of course it could have taken hours.
Wasn't the falling to the bottom enough?
She served her purpose, born knowing.

Time for her was nothing,
darkened silence for her was nothing.

She was born in it.

In wild hives of wild bees,
each one waits until nearly death
to see the world. The last job she takes
being 'The Forager.'

Before that,
only the darkness and the smell of her
brothers and sisters. Only the food.
Only the buzzing of wings.

Wouldn't that make life beautiful?

Seeing and smelling it all for the first time—
knowing it to be true just long enough
to catch your breath and fall.

Landing in someone's
hand, into the bottom
of someone's planter
and letting yourself die—
what did her life mean?

Where did it go?

Into the sun,
to begin again.

Into my witness to remind me
I shouldn't just be here writing.

But let myself out into the light
for the first time so that
I might be breathing, being and
knowing what I was born to know.

And then hands touch—
I skip into the water, catch my breath,
And die.

The Suddenness

It's May here in Kentucky
and the insects have grown closer,
louder and more numerous.

I hear them breathing, calculating
the temperature, singing softly
through a rumble in their whole bodies.

I notice them when they begin
and end—like the suddenness of
leaves on trees.

They are my closest ocean.

When they come home, I catch my
breath.

The Last Month

I am falling in love with August.

Falling leaves (just a few shed) in mix with
a pattering of butterfly wings in the air.

Strawberries are ripe, peaches are ripe,
cherries are ripe. I too am ready.
Fruition has come, but only part of fruiting
is fruit.

After all, it's what comes after. After all,
it never stops.

Change swells up in the throat of the earth.
We are all at the crux of the seasons. August.
Sometimes not hot at all.

A dragonfly slaps into my windshield. I watch
children play. There is a breeze. The trees outside
look fuller, there is no chance they're hollow.
I wait. We all do.

It's a short time, August.

Cockroach
    For River

She told me about the bug on her
floor roughly the size of her pinky.
She didn't know what it was, she insisted.
Maybe I would. She would send me a photo.

She says when she is scared by something,
like this 2 ½ inch bug, her inner ear vibrates,
uncontrollably. A warning, a rumble.
Whatever scares off the birds before a storm.

She calls her son in, and he removes the bug for her.
I tell her I think it's a cockroach. She thinks she should
kill it. How else to keep it from coming back inside?
I say that I just throw mine off the balcony.

It used to be I would ignore them.
Too bothered by them to give even acknowledgment.
Then, after a while, I would scoop them with a little cup
and paper.
Now, since I've gotten to know them, I pick them up with
my bare hands. They are fast though, like mice.
You have to be careful.

Her son, at first believes him dead. And then realizes in
a jump he is not. He takes him outside. He kills him.

  She says,
      "I moved closer to it even though
      my ear drums were vibrating."

A State of Being Near Nightfall

The clouds are pink with atmosphere.

The trees black with shadow.

Sky fades—dusk.

The leaves hang and move like an animal.

Wind beats through them.

Somewhere, in a chair, my head folds sideways into my hand and I listen.

Insects are everywhere.

Cars whir.

Birds, few, and gentle.

Everywhere sound.

Softness too—this that comes with almost night.

Some that are singular, some that are not.

Twilight: civil, nautical, astronomical

If you want to know *fleeting*,
know twilight.

If each of our feelings passed
as quickly as these,
oh, how we would want for them.

In just an act of breathing,
a moment given
staring off into space, it's gone.

And we realize blackness.
We wonder, *if I hold out my hand,
will it be there?*

An insect is crying out
from beyond—one—
and then suddenly,
they all are.

Your House, A Room

There are times when you may sit awake
some hour of the night and realize yourself
sitting there, alone, with only lamp light
and shadows with you in the room.

It will be so stark and clear that your apartment
is really just a room in a house.
With four other rooms and four other lives
occasionally coughing, fucking, and yelling or playing loud
music.

The dust will have settled on the surfaces of your things,
going nowhere just as you are.
Life will seem smaller and more impossible.
Light will fade so that there is just enough for
Darkness to exist.

Portrait Of A Life, Yesterday
For Wren

My dog was with me, pacing in the night.
She cannot see very well for an animal.

Today, she sits with me on the chair,
stretches her neck out, points her head
into the sky, and wiggles her perceptive
little nose. I know what she is doing.

I have done it too.

We have come, she and I—in the early dawn,
to touch our noses to the sky and feel.
Suddenly, we might disappear.
Nothing beyond or below.

I recognize the same things—
The no space—between myself, my dog,
the air, that tree, the gate in the middle of the
night, the perfectly still lake water, reflecting;
the stars woven through some spirit of a cloud.
Clouds at night.

Between me and that toad I released into the wild
there. Between me and my crying at the end of the path.
Between the phone and the phone call.

What is it like to trust a friend?

Like reeds swaying at the edge of the pond.
My dog shoves her big head into my chest.
She knows.

I Must Lay Back into This World

Our last day on the beach
the sun's rays splay out on the
water just like in the paintings
and the terns go fishing just
ten feet off the shore.

The sun's warmth is subtle,
but still unafraid.
To notice it is devotion.

I do, I do, I do.

My dog steps her clumsy foot
into my coffee as she
reaches and reaches around,
tangled by her leash,
looking for life upon the beach.

We have done it.

We have escaped what before
felt utterly inescapable.

I push my forehead against the dirty
forehead of my dog.
We sway, becoming in the morning
air. The salt inside the wind.

It is so beautiful here.

The sunlight hanging in the closet
with the clothes.

The birds singing without
effort in the yard.

The dog curled on the bed,
resting. Her hair still smells like
beach water, though we are
miles and miles from it now.

The plants are green. The air cool
and breathless.

I am home again.

Clawfoot Tub

The water is hot and clean.

I submerge, letting my heavy head
tap smoothly against the porcelain
or whatever it is.

Blood is pushed hard through
the thin casing of each vein
and I beat like a drum—

When I breach, facing the surface,
hair hung down like seaweed,
wet and dark, my breathing
is certain and fast.

Nothing knows the pleasure of breath
like those pelagic mammals—
somehow not fish.

Each rises from some deep and causes
a great lifting of weight,
just tons of water
displaced out from underneath them—
shoved through a blowhole—

"Here I am." Declared and simple.

It doesn't have to be complicated.

When I rise out of the two feet of tub,
I have struck down into something.
Some kind of treasure in the sand.
I can see clearer and feel inside myself,

And I notice I don't stop anywhere.

I look through the thin sliver of window
in my bathroom and see the many leaflets of
the Honey Locust
and I think about those long spindles of
seed pods frail and smacking against my deck.

Soon they will grow and fall down
and I will go out and sweep them off my balcony
and think of how they fall all the way from the tops
of trees and there they lay
hoping to go to seed
and I sweep them off into the grass
and they don't care.

They don't care where they are.

They're always going to be who they
came here to be.

Untitled

Oh, to be that young black dog
running long and wild across the
country lawns and over hills to
chase the fleeting birds away.

Maria Tori is a Japanese-American poet, painter, and bird lover. She has been published in *Poetry East, The Louisville Review, samfiftyfour,* and others. Tori was invited to speak at Spalding Universities' annual 'Outstanding Undergraduate Creative Writers' evening hosted by their MFA program and 21c Hotel and Museum. This is her first published chapbook of poetry.

She resides in Louisville, Kentucky where she studies Environmental Science and Biology with hopes to get a PhD in Coastal Ecology and Ornithology. She lives with her beloved dog, Georgia, who reminds her to be authentic, curious, and assertive every day.

www.ingramcontent.com/pod-product-compliance
Lightning Source LLC
Chambersburg PA
CBHW022129090426
42743CB00008B/1064